*L*ife is a book...

*pages of days sewn together
with laughter and tears;
as an invisible pen leaves our
mark on each hour's line.*

*The moment before
this writing is water already
under the bridge.*

WATER UNDER MY BRIDGE

A Reservoir of Uncommon Common Sense

By

ELLIE NEWBAUER

Cover of Lake Gaston, NC, by the author

&

2013

Wellspring Press

Water Under My Bridge
A Reservoir of Uncommon Common Sense
By Ellie Newbauer
Copyright © 2013, by the author

Book designed by
Judy Knowlton, the Bookbuilder

Available through

www.createspace.com/4479574

and

www.amazon.com

or directly from the Publisher:

Wellspring Press
115 Magnolia Court,
Littleton, NC, 27850
ellienewbauer@gmail.com
2013

For my children,

John, Nancy, Jay and Jill

Our children are ours for a little while,
on loan from God as our master teachers.

Acknowledgments

How in the world do you go about acknowledging all the people that have had an influence in your life? They are the ones who actually wrote this book, not the words but the learning that lives in it.

First were my parents who taught me discipline and my early thoughts and feelings. My siblings who showed me my pecking order and made sure I stayed there. John, the love of my life, who traveled the road with me through thick and thin as we both learned that the road is not always smooth. I am ever grateful to my children, for being my greatest teachers and my dearest joy.

A million thanks to Becky Allen for putting commas and periods where they belonged and encouraging me to be vulnerable. And the same thanks to Judy Knowlton for the hours she spent birthing this book and holding my hand along the way.

And last but far from least is my writing group, especially Arlene Bice, our teacher who knows how to encourage and share her wisdom gently, and Maggie Chalifoux for being the second pair of eyes that found changes to be made in this book and who taught me the difference between "and" and "but"— a most important lesson. My deepest thanks to all of you and the many friends that held my hand...with gratitude and love—

Ellie

Contents

Looking Back	1
Water Under My Bridge	2
Preface	11

Part 1 - Relationships ~ 15

Life's Play	17
Me, Myself, and I	19

Marriage — 21

The Thick and Thin of It	22
Only the Brave Advance	25
Safe Harbor	27
Widow or Artist	29
What Does a Woman Want?	30

Children — 33

Job Interview	34
A Child's Laugh	36
The Dreaded NO	37

Our Family	39
Family's Book of Rights	40
No String Attached	43
The Authorities	45
Teen Years	46
Success or Failure	51
Did I Tell You?	52
Friends	55
Bone Comfortable	57
Pigeonholing	59
Did I Tell You?	60
Plants, Pets, and Other Things	62
Home	64
Our House	65
Did I Tell You?	67
Communication	69
The Spoken Word	70
Conflict	71
My Sister Rose	74
Portraits	76
Freaked	78

PART 2 — ART of SELFISHNESS

The Art of Selfishness	83
The Nature of Things	84
Individuality	86
Drought	88
Walking Robots	89
Kindness Misunderstood	91
Purpose	93
Creators	95
The Ego Journey	97
Here Comes the Judge	100
The Craft Show	103
Water Under the Bridge	106
Reflections	108
Permission Slips	109
Procrastination	111
Straddling the Fence	113
The List Maker	115
The Dream Life	118
Security	119

The Art of Change	121
Self-Awareness	123
Strengths and Weaknesses	124
Facts Are Facts	126
Discontent	127
Starting Point	129
Choosing	130
Forgiving	132
Blinded	135
What I Have Learned	136

Part 3 - FINDING SELF~141

Maturing with Grace	143
The Grubbies	146
The Simple Things	148
Finding Myself	151
Memory Box	153
Doing What is Natural	156
Did I Tell You?	158
Work in Progress	162

$\mathcal{P}$ART 4 — AGING 163

Life's Vacuum	165
Compensations	167
Transient Youth	168
Our Bodies	169
Reflections	171
Ageless	172
Tomorrow's Seed	173
Some Last Thoughts	174

Ellie Newbauer, Biography   175

Looking Back

    I finally found out that life is not a roadmap, all drawn with clear interstates and side roads; but rather a blank that we get to draw our own interstates with side roads of mistakes and successes. And I found that we all leave pieces and parts of ourselves along that road; it's a part of living.

It is said that hindsight is twenty-twenty…that is so true…if I knew then what I know now, life would have been different…but I didn't and it wasn't, so here I am.

Water under my bridge:

I spent the first eight years of my life on a farm in Harborcreek, Pennsylvania with summer fields to run through and mud to squish between my toes on rainy days. But with nine kids in our family chores were not a choice but an expectation. I have to say that farm life is not just grazing cows in a pristine pasture conveyed by writers and artists ... someone's got to milk those cows and feed them; and someone has to cut and bale the hay that they eat.

Because of this I feel I have to set the records straight:

Country Living

*In country journals living is clever, but
somehow I feel these writers have never:*

*milked a cow, slopped a sow,
or walked a mile behind a plow.*

*Shoveled manure, lived without sewer,   or
had to get ready for the hams to cure.*

*Pulled the weed, filled bins with feed, and
hoped that Sears would send the seed.*

*Pitched the hay, cursed the day, or
wondered why the chickens won't lay.*

   Nor have they ever - - -

*Watched the sun set on a fresh ploughed
field,*

*smelled the damp earth and dreamed of its
yield.*

*Felt gentle rain when the fields were so
dry,*

with a feeling of gratitude money can't buy.
   Or

*Seen rows of jars, each with a label,
a flock of kids round a full dining table.*

*These are the things I remember we did
when we lived on the farm and I was a kid.*

Time has a way of moving on. The great depression of 1929 came and went leaving our lives changed forever. Two brothers, Byron and Grant died of polio and the four oldest, Rose, Allen, Eva and Louise, married moving into homes of their own, leaving the three youngest, me, Bill, and Chuck.

I was eight, Bill seven, Chuck five the spring that Mom and Dad piled the three of us into an old Ford touring car and drove away from the bitter cold of Erie, heading south, leaving behind the pasture, creek, and fields that I knew by heart. Dad had a new job waiting for him in D.C., a true answered prayer in the mid depression years; it paid twenty five dollars a week, a fortune in 1933, and was our way to a better life.

We moved into a furnished flat on the second floor of a row house that had seen better days...much better...but it became home for the five of us for a time.

Being the new kid on the block is never easy. I was not only new but city ways were beyond me. I had no idea that you could buy ice cream in a store; I thought it was churned in the yard on a summer Sunday. Neither did I know what Coca-

Cola was...cider was the closest I'd ever come to a specialty drink.

The neighborhood kids acted like I was from Mars and I began to wonder about that. I stopped being so forthcoming about what I didn't know and waited to see what they did, then, did the same. After a while they stopped looking at me in disbelief as the strange kid in the neighborhood, and I became used to city ways.

October 3, 1942, four months into my seventeenth year I married John, the love of my life; he was nineteen. We were married by the justice of the peace in Ellicott City, Maryland along with our best friends, Tommy and Ruth. The secretary to the justice was the only witness. The ceremony took about twenty minutes and was over by noon. That afternoon the four of us moved into an attic apartment no bigger than a shoe box, pretending to be worldly wise grown-ups. In hindsight we were babies hardly dry behind the ears.

World war two was raging. The certainty that John would be drafted into the service hung like a cold fog. Just three months after our wedding day the dreaded letter came, "John Joseph Newbauer has been selected..."

John left for navy boot-camp …it was January of 1943.

I grew up fast that year. My allotment as a service man's wife was fifty dollars a month, not enough to afford our attic hide-away, so I had to move back home with Mom and Dad. Bill and Chuck were still living at home and I guess I thought that life would pick up where I left it three months before as a carefree teen. That didn't happen. In my family once you marry you are considered grown and I was expected to get a job…immediately and pay room and board.

I set out the next day fully expecting to have a job by days end. I was stunned when, after the required physical, I was told I was pregnant and not employable. This was a pivotal moment in my life; one that determined the better part of my future.

The hardest thing I ever had to do was tell my Dad that I was going to have a baby. I'm not sure what I expected, guilt maybe, but his only comment then, or ever, was, "we can work it out." I don't know why that was such a relief, but it was. In that moment I learned appreciation down to my toes. I also learned that dads are not just law and order but have big hearts that turn to mush when their kid needs them.

That was when my understanding of responsibility and how much I depended on others grew beyond my childness. I was learning fast that the time comes when you are not owed anything, but are given to out of the goodness of others.

John Joseph Newbauer lll was born eight months later, and it didn't take him long to wrap his tiny fingers around every heart in that house.

Dad's dream was to live in Florida where he thought it was always warm and every day was sunny. The opportunity came for him when a job opening was announced in Pensacola, which he accepted.

It was taken for granted by both Mom and Dad that the baby and I would go with them; but the very thought about what I had heard of the heat and bugs made me shudder; It was the last place I wanted to live.

Even though my government allotment had been raised to eighty dollars a month when Johnny was born, it was still not enough to rent a place and care for a new baby. But the thought of going south made me queasy; I couldn't imagine it, and I struggled to think of some way not to go.

I was telling my sister, Rose, about my dilemma and mentioned a $600 dollar check that John had sent home for deposit in a savings account. (It seems there were not many places for a sailor to spend a pay check in New Guiney during a war).

That's when she said, "Why don't you buy a house with that money as down payment? I thought her crazy as a loon…but, it didn't take us long to come up with a plan that seemed workable. She would move in with me and pay the rent she was paying for her apartment. There would be enough with her rent money and my allotment to pay the mortgage, the utilities and feed the three of us…no frills, but believe me I wasn't looking for frills.

I found a brick two bedroom cottage which would be perfect, but it presented a big problem. The house cost $6,500 and required a 10% down payment. I was $50 short of the $650 required and I didn't know where to turn; no one I knew had $50 to spare or was willing to take a chance on such an idea.

I decided to simply face the realtor and tell the truth. With heart in hand I told him my story, particularly the fact that Florida held no appeal for me what so ever, and it was the last place in the world I wanted to live.

The realtor made a phone call to the powers that be, and when he finished his expression said it all; they would accept my $600 for the down payment!

So, instead of depositing the six hundred dollars, I bought a house.

I was eighteen when Rose, Johnny and I moved into 207 Monroe Avenue, Alexandria, Virginia...our new home.

I was so excited that I forgot to be afraid.

"Oh, my God," was all Mom could get out. She worried about how I would take care of everything, especially a nine-month old baby, without her.

I, in my young-bravado, didn't give it a second thought. It was summer of 1944.

Rose and I settled into our new life together, she going to work and me staying home as a mom and housekeeper. Going to work for me was not an option, for at that time, there were no pre-schools or nurseries to care for the babies of working mothers. So I settled into my make-believe life with my little house and baby, but in reality it was a daily waiting for news and letters. It was like holding your breath, not knowing what the day would bring. Everyone and everything was in a holding pattern waiting for the war to end so that life could start again.

The war finally ended in the fall of 1945 and John came home...home to a house, baby and wife he didn't know. It is funny how in one day your entire life turns a corner and nothing is ever the same.

The day John came home, Johnny was one month shy of two years old and knew only me as his world of security. He was not at all receptive to the stranger in his house whose name was Daddy, and he wanted nothing to do with him, which was understandable but very disappointing.

Life picked up, seemingly where we had left it as newly-weds; except we were three years older and strangers to the new people that we each had become. That, too, was understandable, unexpected and disillusioning.

Our marriage was not perfect by any stretch of the imagination, but we stayed together through thick and thin for fifty eight years.

Those, and the twelve years since John's death are the fodder for these uncommon common sense thoughts.

Preface

I got up every morning, put on my shoes and did what had to be done to fill most needs, mine as well as others; still do. That is a given. That is a privilege. Even so, I felt there had to be something more to life than this; but every time that thought came up the grouchy judge living inside me cringed. His job was to keep my feet to the fire of daily duty, God forbid that I did anything frivolous or daring during the hours that were set aside for daily work.

Nevertheless, I, in my illegal non-productiveness, love to splash words all over the page letting them fall into whatever they decide to become. That's when the judge waves an invisible finger, admonishing me for wasting time.

Sometimes I have to muffle that damn judge. I would really like to bury the grouch; he's not always right and is a pain in the lower extremities.

It took me longer than seems necessary to find that I'm good at some things and not so good at others. This you would think would be branded in your psyche at birth, but it isn't, or if it is, mine was lost in the shuffle. It didn't dawn as a light bulb moment either, but took time and more fizzles than I care to count. I was seeing silver among the gold in my hair before I realized I was a teacher, a mentor and a want-to-be writer.

My writing lay fallow for years. I wrote notebooks full of thoughts and poetry and shoved them into a drawer where they gathered dust, while the judge mumbled his disapproval. Today I pulled them all out, and despite a screaming sink of dirty dishes, I kept my behind in a chair and my writing in sight...daring the judge in me to whisper a word.

This book is a gathering of that collection.

Words tumble onto the page,
like rain down a spout...
sometimes soft,
sometimes stumbling
one over the other
in their rush to be heard...
leaving behind
a trough of debris.

&

Part 1

Relationships

Give me the wisdom to know when I have my nose where it doesn't belong, the good sense to remove it, and the courage to tell others to do the same.

Life's Play

The people in our lives are tools given to us to create experiences; our responses become our book of history.

☙

Relationships are something we all need, unless you're a cave dwelling hermit in Timbuktu. We seek people to share our days, wanting them to recognize that we exist. It's satisfying when they commiserate with us on our bad days and laugh with us on our good ones, but what is more important, is that they see us, and hear us, and respond to us.

We bring people into our lives with every personality and temperament imaginable just so we can experience the connection and the effect they have on us. Sounds kinky until you think about it; without them we wouldn't have anything to compare ourselves to.

I have to agree with Shakespeare, life is a play and the people that drop in fit their roles like a glove; some are easy and move through our lives with hardly a missed cue, while others are more difficult. Those who are difficult give us a fit because they don't follow their script the way we want them to. We want them to be what we want them to be, do what we want them to do, the way we want them to do it, and give us what we want when we want it. And when that doesn't happen, they become our antagonist and a story line in our play.

Relationships are just that...relating to people and things through the feelings of attachment we have, and what we do about them.

As David Seabury wrote:

"You are not a victim of the world, but rather a participant in its creation through the role you play in it."

Me, Myself, and I

After all is said and done, we three, me, myself and I, will be the last ones standing with all our mistakes and success written all over us.

☙

In one of my brooding moments I came to a jarring thought. I realized that I am the only one that is with me every moment of every day and the only one that is going to be with me forever. Everyone else is going to leave me sooner or later.

All four children, John, Nancy, Jay and Jill, filled my daily thoughts and activities for years, becoming my life's reason for being. But in time they grew up and away, and moved into lives and homes of their own. That was the ultimate goal-—to have independent adults in place of the dependent, insecure children I bore.

They all finished their job, teaching me the art of nurturing; and I finished mine, teaching the importance of being nurtured; and when our jobs were done, they left, and I turned another corner.

John, the love of my life for fifty eight years, died. The fact is that a spouse or significant other, or I, will move on whether by death, divorce or choice. We all leave behind a myriad of memories, some good, some not; their effects are indelibly imprinted on that which we have become.

Our friends, even those we are closest to, move out of our life for one reason or another. But they have instilled in us the knowing of camaraderie and acceptance, and we are different because we have known them.

Along with everyone else, even those who are a pain in the behind, disappear sooner or later, leaving behind a residue to wonder about...how did they serve me in my learning?

☙

Did I tell you that the most important relationship in your life, by far, is the one you have with yourself?

☙

Did I tell you that you are the only one that is with you every second of every hour of every day forever, no matter what? And you make all of your decisions...creating life as you see it?

☙

Marriage

The love held for a child, sister or friend is different than that held by lovers for each other...or is it...

...surely there is the want in lovers to nurture and protect one another as though a beloved child...

to have the closeness that allows secrets to flow between them as if to a trusted sister...

to have the love of one friend for another in the camaraderie of day to day living and laughing.

But when the heart beats faster at the sound of the other's footfall, when there's anticipation of another's touch or word and when a light shines for the other alone...that is when two hearts flow together, creating a world not known to any other.

The Thick and Thin of It

*Two hearts walk a sacred path
as together they find their way
through the brambles.*

☙

There is a lot of thick and thin in staying married to the same man for fifty-eight years, and sometimes the thin outweighed the thick for both of us. That's when some hefty repair work was called for, and it took a long time to learn how to keep those thin places from tearing wide open. Those lean times can't be patched with meaningless conversations, which only hide resentment, hurt feelings and anger; that patch will tear away leaving a gaping hole. Each one need to be recognized, considered and heard, not blown off like a piece of lint, in the hopes the problem will go away. Sounds reasonable, so why is it so hard?

After a lot of gaping holes I have come to understand that it has to do with intimacy/vulnerability; which is a scary place for the ego to explore.

It's hard to lay yourself open when you're afraid you might be left in a pool of rejection. That takes courage. Instead we pussyfoot around the real problem by bringing up all kinds of old undigested hang-ups, either out loud or in the silence of our minds. The real trouble goes untouched while we focus on why someone didn't take out the garbage or why someone did what they did last month; these are blinders that keep us from the hurting place...where the real issue lives.

Our hurting place is where we shove the longing to be assured, to be important enough to be heard, not only by others but by ourselves. Have you ever noticed that we sometimes talk to our pets better than we do ourselves...what's up with that?

These hurting places become sore spots that we ignore, hoping at best that they go away and at the least they won't show. They don't go away; they just sits there and hurt like hell. Vitality seeps out with the longing, and the relationship dries up; the people in it start living together apart...pretending strangers breathing the same dead air, as each turns somewhere else to fill the longing to belong.

Exploring the hurting places is tricky. It takes a lot of tongue control to keep the truth from turning into blaming. That's when courage seems to come from some unnamed place inside where our soul is crying to be heard.

Did I tell you that having the determination to stand in one's authenticity and integrity is the adhesive that binds relationships? They make the relationship worth having...or not having, if the other can't find honor in that.

Only the Brave Advance

I stayed in a settled-for marriage fifty-six years too long. Don't mistake "settled-for" as bad. Far from it, our marriage was not bad; it just avoided how good it could have been.

John had a mistress. Her name was work. And I couldn't... no I wouldn't... compete with her because she supported us and we all depended on her. But John fell in love, working night and day to appease her. I didn't complain much even though I knew and hated watching him spend so much time with her. But she paid our bills, and so I settled.

Now in all fairness to her, I have to say, she was attractive and interesting with some new tease every day. I never demanded what I wanted like she did. She asked loud and clear, and he filled her every demand with even more than asked for. That's when she proclaimed him wonderful by giving him promotions, and with each promotion he fell deeper in love. I should have nipped this romance in the bud when I first became aware of it, but I didn't. I didn't know that was part of my job.

This sounds like a whiny saga, but not so. As I said in the beginning, I am finding pieces and parts of myself that I've left along the way, and this happens to be one that socked me between the eyes. Not that John was a workaholic...we all knew that, but that I condoned it by taking full advantage of the results. I have never looked at this situation like this before, and wonder how many others are making the same mistake...letting overwork rule their lives by either doing it or taking advantage of it?

John was as honest as the day was long, a good man, and I loved him mightily. If I'd had the boldness that I have today you can bet that mistress would've had a run for her money---oh yeah!

Safe Harbor

The day-to-day sharing of the same bed, same bathroom, same toaster, same everything can, every once-in-awhile, get old...it's that if-he-says-that-one-more-time-I'll-scream kind of feeling. That's when I knew it was time for me to leave...to get away from him, this house, and these kids for a few days.

 I knew I was on the right track when everyone cheered as they saw the back-end of my car leaving for a couple of days "to check on the lake house". Secretly, I did them one better; I drove away singing with gusto, the radio volume turned to blow-the-speakers pitch. I was like a three year old in a sand box filled with toys.

That feeling lasted for almost a week while the heaviness inside me melted. The relief was palpable.

As good as those days were the time always came when I started to miss the familiar, the sweetness of the same bed, the same bathroom, the same toaster, and I began feeling antsy. I was at loose ends in not doing my job of mothering, wife-ing and house-keeping.

Coming back to the familiar smell and feel of home was deeply satisfying, and everyone, even the house, was glad to see me come through the door.

&

Did I tell you that I am campaigning to have uninterrupted self-time written into the marriage vows along with love and honor?

&

Widow or Artist

Couples who are joined at the hip are crippled in more ways than one.

☙

Several months after John died, I met Mary Wilkenson, a neighbor, while walking, and as is the custom, she asked how I was. I said the usual "fine", which should have ended that. But Mary was anything but usual and gave me the look of one who has been where I was. Then she said something that I have never forgotten. She said, "When Bill died I decided that I could be a widow or I could be an artist. I *chose* to be an artist." That's it. Without another word, she just walked away. That was a one minute delay in my walk that changed the rest of my life.

I decided then and there not to be a widow, but rather a writer and mentor, leaving a bit of myself behind so that when I die it would cause a bit of a stir.

☙

What Does a Woman Really Want?

Ages ago at a cocktail party a man with tongue in cheek (or maybe one martini too many) asked me, "What does a woman really want from her man?" I don't remember my reply and I dare say, neither does he, but it made me think...what would I want in a man?

First, I would want a friend. A friend is comfortable. I can say what I am feeling and thinking, share my ideas and dreams and he wouldn't make me feel silly, give a dismissive yawn, or worse, go fish-eyed. And he would feel secure in sharing his innermost thoughts with me, knowing they would be held sacred and in secret.

Second, if this were my husband, I would want an equal partnership——someone to discuss ideas, situations and thoughts with, no matter how personal, and feel secure in their consideration. He would know that listening is as active and vital to our discussion as talking. There would be an acknowledgement that I had been heard and closure if the situation called for it. If an agreement was not reached, we would compromise, or at the very least, agree to disagree. But for goodness sake, I need to have some kind of closure; nothing is worse than a dangling discussion. If I don't know where I stand or what to expect it leaves me feeling half-heard or not heard at all.

Third, I would certainly want someone I could trust. Without trust friendships are frail. Who would want to spill their guts to someone and then hear it from someone else next week, or find that you were told a bald face lie or that you agreed on something and then he forgot to remember?

I bet if that man had asked any woman at that party the same question he would've pretty much gotten the same answer. I dare say this description would fit most women's dream man or woman, as the case may be.

Did I tell you that problems not handled as they come up, multiply like rabbits?

☙

Did I tell you that most people, especially our spouses, are not mind-readers? We act as though they should know what we want simply by the fact that we exist, and then we sulk if they don't get it right?

☙

Did I tell you that asking for what you want works a whole lot better than waiting around for someone else to make up their mind what you will have?

☙

Did I tell you to marry for what the other IS... not what you NEED him/her to be?

☙

Children

CONCEPTION

How is it to know, this tiny speck,
that there is a breath, a beat,
a song to sing,
as stars hang waiting,
and the door to everywhere is opened?

How is it to know, this tiny speck,
that to satisfy the holy within it
dreams are stolen from heaven,
as a window swings wide,
awaiting its song?

Job Interview

Could you imagine applying for a job that has a description like this?

Wanted: parents:

- Full time (24 hrs. a day, 7 days a week)
- Willing to give up life, limb and mental faculty
- Be willing to lose sleep, dignity and the sense of self
- Supply the wherewithal to keep body and soul of another together
- Required to be a nurse, counselor, psychologist, teacher, chauffeur, fashion coordinator and chief cook and bottle washer
- Training helpful, but on the job training available
- Cost of start-up and maintaining, unpredictable

- Job has unlimited potential, depending on degree of involvement of twenty years or so

- Bonuses given periodically, such as pride, confidence, knowledge, strength, companionship, and a heart overflowing with a lifetime of love

- Retirement benefits: the possibility of a best friend for life.

A Child's Laugh

A child's laugh is like the wind,
where does it come from,
where does it go?
Is it waiting in the never-never,
to be caught by a passing
brook,
sing its song
and move on?

The Dreaded NO

A mother of any species will give her life for her child, but sometimes in the heat of battle I wonder why.

☙

I believe babies are born smarter than any two parents, and from their very first breath they set their course to take over. This is their plan: they let you think you are in charge and appear innocent as they wrap themselves around your heart, filling it with such love that every thought will be of them. Once they have your heart they will work on your common sense. These little ones are smart; they know just how to handle us, and they are cruel. They make us commit to a lifetime of love that is so deep that we are willing to die for them.

We must not allow these innocents to invade our common sense...our hearts, yes, but common sense has to be kept as our only defense. From the very beginning we find ourselves giving in on the slippery slope of their wheedling. We must put our foot down and use the dreaded "no".

The slide begins slowly, without notice, but gains momentum as we give in and become the bottomless provider of their every whim. Young kids are the most dangerous because they can convince us that we're their hero and can make anything happen. It's those little things that lull us into an unwavering desire to please them and prove them right. As time goes by and they grow, so do their wants. It's not until they are teens that we realize how far down the slope we've slid. By then we have to fight for our sanity.

Sounds like kids are monsters that we need to avoid at all cost. Not so. John and I survived four different forays into parenthood, and although covered with battle scars, I have to say, they were the best, most loving years of our lives.

Our Family

There are four siblings in this family of ours,

Born to the same mother, and same father,

and lived in the same house, and saw the same places,

and played the same games, and had the same secrets,

and were spanked, And were loved,

grew up and left home...

each so very different.

Four became seven as three married,

then there were separations, and coming together,

and crying, and laughing, and hating and loving...

☙

Family's Book of Rights

Good parenting deserves a standing ovation for the performance...a skill that not everyone comes by easily. For most, it is trial and error and the hope that we are not doing major damage to our child's psyche.

☙

Solidarity between the parents brings security. Being wishy-washy doesn't cut it. Those kids will play you like a fiddle, pitting parent against parent, and when you play that game they have you in the palm of their hand.

Kids are not mature. *They know only what feels good in the moment,* never thinking beyond that. If left to their own whims they lose out when one day they wake in an unfamiliar world that holds them accountable.

A child's familiar world of home is the safest training ground for responsibility and self-discipline. Children, as well as parents, feel more secure when the consequences of actions are known beforehand. These are to be written as the *family's book of rights*, written in indelible ink and used as a guide book for the whole family.

Every child born is different. Each one comes into this world encoded with their specific pattern, personality and needs, but unfortunately there are no directions attached. That is when parenting becomes a challenge and we have to rely on our common sense and an intuitive heart to put it all together, and hope to goodness that we get it right.

Finding ourselves on the slippery slope of placing a kid's wants *before the family's well-being* is a big mistake, one that could spell disaster. This is where "The Family Book of Rights" is a life saver...literally.

Parents are old children, but with the huge responsibility to show the way to their young. They teach what they know, and if they haven't learned self-discipline, the family is in trouble. Nobody knows what to expect; chaos takes over and family life goes to hell in a hand basket.

Parenting children is an undertaking that has no guarantees. Kids do not come with guarantees, so the final outcome is often out of our hands. We hope and pray for the best, and do the best we know to instill all the right values, but the final outcome is the individual child's choosing. We cannot determine what is best for another's soul needs, or what lives in another's heart, even the heart of our beloved child.

༄

Being a parent is the most awesome job any individual could undertake. It is fraught with insecurities, and the feeling of inadequacy will bring you to your knees. Then something happens, like your kid stands in the truth when the odds are against him or her, and you feel your heart so full of pride that tears spring from nowhere.

༄

No String Attached

We plow into life, praying that our rows will be straight and deep enough; then we plant our dreams and wait for the harvest.

☙

Every one of our four kids is different. What worked for one didn't work for the other, and it took all we had to figure out who needed what, and when. We weren't always successful, in fact we missed as often as not.

For instance, I could never wrap my thinking around our third child's chaotic world and haphazard life; still can't, even now in his mid-years. Our eyes look into two different worlds, and we each find the other's untenable.

For years my thought was to change him so that he would fit into the world as I saw it, where he would be safe and secure. That didn't work at all and just turned into a big fat mess.

He wears his world like his skin, as I do mine. I can't crawl inside him anymore than he could live inside of me. So where does that leave us? Just where we are...two people that love one another mightily and want to be a part of each other's life and to be accepted just the way we are, with no strings attached.

I still want him to be safe and secure in my world; but I know that is not for him and never will be.

&

Did I tell you that the trouble with having kids is that you fall in love with them just as they are and then set about trying to change them...

&

The Authorities

Our kids all have a great funny bone. I didn't know that until they were half grown. I was busy reading every book and listening to every Tom, Dick, and Harry that touted the latest on how to raise a child from the first gassy smile until "I do" at the altar.

I convinced myself that these "authorities" knew more than I about caring for our kids, and I was sure that I would be labeled a rotten mother and they would be doomed to a life of bumhood if they didn't fit the mold.

Turned out those "authorities" didn't know any more, or, as much as I did. I found out that it is impossible to stuff four different personalities into the same mold; that makes a mess that's hard to clean up.

Teen Years

*I am convinced that the teen years
are a conspiracy by God to break the ties
that are so binding. Overnight the teen can
become a monster and parents a babbling
knot of frustration...*

&

I Remember

Behind closed doors the teenager lives

with TV, stereo and anything that gives

pleasure to their eye, their ear, their tongue,

keeping you on edge, hung up, unstrung..

They seem so aloof, in a world their own,

Their tongue they have learned just how to hone

so that it rips and tears and leaves you in shreds,

and every encounter fills you with dread.

Take heart, mom and dad, the time's sure to come

when the fridge will be stocked and there are some

cokes in the pantry, chips, dip and bread,

the tops on the mayo, the cheese is not dead.

The beds will be made, the garbage in place,

not in a night stand forming a case

of mold that would send a germ in a tizzy,

and you'll be relieved, the phone won't ring busy.

Hold onto your faith and your good senses,

when your female child is in her menses.

She is finicky, miniky, picky and proud,

nothing is right she lives in a shroud

that leaves the house dreary, teary and sad,

the weekend is shot, everyone's mad.

You wonder, "why do I put up with this?"
then she'll turn round and give you a kiss
on the cheek and says, "I'm sorry, Mom,
I feel so ugly, so gangly, so dumb".
Your eyes will fill, your heart will melt,
as you remember just how you felt
when you were a teen and all was drear,
you hated yourself when you looked in the mirror.
Your hair was limp, complexion blah,
and every day a new zit you saw.
At times the female teen is not fun,

but wait,
what do you think of your teen age son,
with his shoes that smell like something rotten,
his underwear under the bed forgotten?
Clean clothes or dirty, they're all in a heap,
it's enough to make a grown woman weep.

And somewhere in this room of his

are magazines full of dirty biz.

Between the sexes I may be torn.

for there are times my son has worn

his heart on his sleeve for me to see,

when I feel in the dumps and want to be free,

He'll hug me tight, and in his way,

"How's it going, Mom", is all he'll say.

Now they are grown and out of this house,

at last there are two, me and my spouse.

"Oh blessed day", I cried with glee,

now there is time for him and me"!

But, wait,

what is this I hear you say,

"It's so quiet through-out the day"

no more slammin' of the door,

or coming home voices that fairly soar,

"what's to eat, I'm really starved".

Memories are strong and they have carved
A place in our heart that fills with glee,
when we visit that which used to be.

&

Success or Failure?

Buried in a mother's heart is a secret knowing about each new gift of life God has placed in her arms. It's true.

҈

There are successes and failures in all of life, and I believe we sometimes become confused as to which is which.

To hear our kids talk you would think we fed them bread and water and beat them hourly. But, in the next breath they talk about the wonderful childhood they had...so did we succeed or fail at parenting? Like all things there seems to be a fine line, depending on the recollection in the moment.

Despite my motherhood fumbling, and finding that the world didn't end every time I made a mistake, all four kids reached adulthood as decent people... people that live in my heart and that I really like and want to spend my time with. That is big time success in my thinking.

҈

Did I Tell You?

Parents are a strange lot. They think of teens as their babies, and yet expect them to act like worldly wise adults.

※

Babies grow into teens testing their wings of independence, fledglings no longer tied to us like chicks in a nest.

※

Have I already told you that letting go was the hardest thing to do?   *It is.*

※

I know all about nature and how a mother bird knows to let her babies spread their wings and become strong in order to survive. But damn it, I'm not a bird, and I still fret when my mid age children make decisions that has disaster written all over them. I want to shout warnings in their ear, but age makes you a bit more restrained, if not less controlling, and so silence has served us both well.

※

I have often asked God why He gave a mother a mother's heart that is torn so easily. I still don't know, but I believe that in every child a piece of that heart lives, showing them how to love unconditionally.

&

Friends

Not all people are worn like familiar clothes that seem to tuck and drape in all the right places, but those who do fit like an old shoe.

Bone Comfortable

Choosing those we call friend is an important happening. They are no longer acquaintances but members of our heart.

☙

Yesterday I had lunch at a lakeside restaurant with Mary, a friend whose intensity is catching. We spent three hovering hours like two schoolgirls tip-toeing into the intimacies of our lives; it was like a good book that you couldn't put down.

It was an interesting happenstance that a group of women gathered at a table nearby. Their laughter and talk tumbled out without a thought, one louder than the next. The contrast between us struck me with how much our needs differ at different times. I loved the intimacy of sharing deeply with a trusted friend, but I have at other times been in a rowdy bunch and added my two cents worth right along with the loudest. Interestingly I came away from both exhilarated and bone comfortable; each serving a deep need.

We all want to belong and belonging is different at different times. When it comes right down to the grit, it's all about liking ourselves and accepting that with grace. I have learned that people like and accept me about as much as I like and accept myself; not a pretend showy liking but rather a knowing and accepting the bad, the good, the ugly and the beautiful. I have come to the realization that it's about the same mix for all of us. It is in that knowing that I can let myself out to society whether it is a one-on-one intimacy or laughing at a bawdy joke.

Pigeonholing

*My best friends were strangers
that I was waiting to meet*

☙

We have a way of compartmentalizing our friends. When I look back I can see where I put my friends in compartments. I had bridge friends, club friends, neighborhood friends, and church friends, all in tidy places in my mind. I spent a lot of time with these people and found it interesting to discover that I let different parts of myself out to each group. They were my connection to the outer world, where I could compare my thinking, reasoning self.

This usually doesn't happen in the family; that is an entirely different dynamic. Our original families take us for granted because we are each other's history, and in time our spouses and children join that place of familiarity. That's why friends are so important; they can give us a sense of ourselves that families cannot.

☙

Did I Tell You?

A friend is someone with open ears
and a shut mouth.

☙

Did I tell you that good friends understand that dust is a part of life; they also understand that sometimes eating ice cream out of the box is all right.

☙

Did I tell you that our relationships tell our inside story...the way we see ourselves? The people we choose to be in our life...friends, partners, associates...all are a reflection of the core beliefs we hold about ourselves.

☙

Did I tell you that it's alright to avoid people whose happiness seems to be in counting the ways of their miseries and sacrifices as though they were being groomed for sainthood?

☙

Did I tell you that close-knit family and friends are those who do a lot of repair work when the fabric of their relationship wears thin?

Did I tell you to be honest with yourself, for you are your best friend, and to lie to your best friend is traitorous?

Plants, Pets, and Other Things

Things have a way of owning us.

☙

Relationships are not just with people but include the things in our life. My cats, house, car, computer, and plants, all are a part of my life and I have an affair with all of them.

For instance my cats, Charley and Jess, certainly have their own personalities and we respond to one another. When I respond to their demands for attention they purr their contentment...but it has to be on their terms. My car, Angelfly, knows how important she is in my life because I tell her so every time we travel together. My plants, most with their own names, grow better when I talk to them and let them know I care.

My computer is a different story. I have no great loyalty to it; in fact, we've had more misunderstandings than I want to remember. If it were not so convenient I would divorce it today. My relationship with it is not good, but I'm working on it.

My writing is another one of those love/hate relationships. I love writing but I hate the uncertainty of the blank staring page.

Our home, The Gathering Place, is my favorite relationship among things, and one that I give a lot of thought to.

Home

A house is a building that is divided into rooms. No matter how large or small, it doesn't become home until, along with the furniture, you move in all the dreams and worries, loving and hating, good times laughed and the sad times cried. Only then does the house become the family's flavor; it becomes the familiar of our lives. A home is the people living in it, whether it is you by yourself or you, a spouse and a passel of kids.

Our House

Our house has windows and doors, and walls and furniture, and sun spilling onto the floor.

There are plants spreading out as if they owned the place, and a recipe box overflowing its treasures.

A muted afghan lays crumpled in the couch corner, along with knitting's red balls of yarn strung to the floor.

There are half filled cups, the brewing still heavy in the air, and books on tables, on shelves, on the floor, mostly with tattered covers, reminders of hours spent in love with words.

The clock ticks, and the floors groan, especially in the stillness of night, and the walls hold sounds of happy birthday sung, children laughing, children crying, and grown-up sounds…some happy, some not.

Sometimes I hear my house whispering in the night's quiet, an occasional mouse sound blends with the rafters that sigh as the wind plays hide and seek at its corners.

Every body's house is different. Some you feel at home the minute you walk in while others feel closed and unfriendly; like someone needs to let out a long held breath. I can't put my finger on it, it's just a feeling...like it's o.k. to nap on the couch or it's not.

&

The smell of a house is the fingerprint of the life lived there.

Some are nice, like cookies baking, Christmas, and ivory soap,

some are like moth balls,
all closed up and tight, reminding me of hand-me-down clothes,

some are like wet dogs and sneakers, stinky but reassuring.

some are not nice, like something forgotten for a very long time.

&

Did I Tell You?

Did I tell you to use your house, every nook and cranny, and take decent care of it? But for goodness sakes, don't let it run your life. It's a home, not a museum or a mausoleum for the dead; It's a place for the living, dreaming, laughing, crying people that live there who need to know that they are prized and that couches are made for napping.

☙

Did I tell you that a clean house is no substitute for lying in the grass with a four year old as elephants float by in the clouds?

☙

Communication

Communication is the backbone of any relationship and comes in many different forms and guises. Words are the foundation of our interaction, but have you ever noticed that the word is often not the message? It is rather in the look, tone or stance used by the speaker, which we seem to pick up by osmosis.

We read one another like a book.

The Spoken Word

The spoken word
  is a mighty storm
    full of destruction
      and tears,

      or

a gentle sigh
  to caress
    a sleeping babe.

Do they gather
  in a distant cloud of life
    to shower us
      in our unaware moments?

Conflict

Disagreements happen: you can't live in this world honestly without them. The diversity of the world depends on these differences. You will find your thoughts and beliefs being opposed; unless you are such a namby-pamby that you put your brain on hold until *someone else* makes up your mind what you want or believe.

If I should count the ways that others don't agree with me, we would miss a lot of meals. But on the other hand, I don't always think others know what they're talking about either.

That reminds me of the time, in my innocent ignorance, that I asked a priest why he said The Lord's Prayer so fast. The instant chill clued me into knowing this was the wrong thing to ask. I was informed in no uncertain terms that his was the way it is to be, and I was not to question.

To this day I don't agree with him, even though he has become bishop, and I'm sure he would still not agree with me. I will continue my slow methodic, time consuming meditation/prayer and he will, in all likely-hood, race through his.

Does it really matter? I don't believe the world would stop or even bat an eye either way. Sometimes you just have to agree to disagree.

There are billions of people in this world and as many ways of seeing things…much of it is leftover history. It doesn't make them right or wrong, but different…that is each one's divine right.

The old saying if you can't beat them join them is a lot of hogwash. I don't like wallowing in someone else's notions, I have enough of my own to keep me busy.

❧

Can you imagine a world where everyone had the exact same thought and belief about the exact same thing at the exact same time? Nothing would get done. There would be nothing new to think about, and I wouldn't be spending a gazillion dollars on new books.

❧

Have I told you, that in relationships, telling yourself and the other that everything is fine when it isn't is a lie, an indescribable treachery? It kills the very force within you and renders you impotent. You cannot make a relationship better or save it by lying to yourself or anyone else. Saying everything is fine when it isn't, is negating your self-worth as well as that of the other.

My Sister Rose

You don't have to fill every moment with conversation, I hear you better when my brain has some digestion time.

☙

Have you ever been with someone that is a non-stop talker? I had a sister like that. I swear she could talk an ear off and start on the other one without missing a beat. I could get a whole week's ironing done, bake a cake, and clean the kitchen in one phone call. An occasional "uh huh" was my contribution, and *that* I had to lay in sideways. The amazing thing is, that when she hung up, I wondered what she had to say, the talk was so non-stop that it disappeared in my distractions.

That was a long time ago, when cutting the conversation short or telling her how I felt, or what I wanted was out of the question. It would have sent her into a tailspin of intimidating self-flagellation for wasting my time; and sent me digging into my guilt-bag of inconsideration.

What a waste of valuable time for both of us; we missed the precious gift of a sister's special sharing of their deepest thoughts and dreams.

When I started liking myself enough to speak up, it was too late...she was gone.

Portraits

*Our tongues paint pictures
for others to see, which becomes
a self-portrait.*

☙

Once in a writing workshop the instructor told us to write our impression of our Mother. It was to be the first thought that came and not more than one sentence. I took him at his word, and I wrote.

After the other's readings of apple pies, sweetness and devotion, I felt like I was going to puncture a sacredness that we dare not touch with earthly feelings. My Mom did the apple pie, sweetness and devotion thing...but my, when she let loose, her tongue was like a whip snapping in the wind.

To say I was apprehensive when it came my time to read was putting it mildly. It was more like a batter knowing the pitch is aimed straight at him and there's nowhere to go...so I read...

*"She had a nutpick tongue
that knew instinctively where to jab
to get the sweetest meat."*

The silence was deafening. Not a sound, until the instructor said, "Well done" and I started to breathe again.

I have thought of that instant impression of my Mother and wonder where it came from. I knew her as the Norman Rockwell type, but obviously there was more to my feeling about her than that. It was my mid-life writing experience in that workshop that shocked me into finding her human. I looked at my Mother differently after that. I realized that she was like everyone else and had feelings, dreams, and opinions...some good and some not good. It dawned on me that she was not just my Mom; she was simply another human being looking for her place in the world, where she could be heard, accepted and loved......what a revelation.

☙

Freaked

Life is a constant quarrel. We want everything to stay the same because it's familiar and we know what to expect. On the other hand, every fiber of our being is saying grow...grow...just try. And if we don't try, the world leaves us in the dust of change.

☙

I wonder what Mom would think if she had a peek into the world of today with its automatic everything. I do believe she would freak out. Her world was a wood cook stove, wringer washer, pencil/paper, broom...and kids that listened when she spoke, in fear of the consequences if we didn't.

I am a bit freaked myself when it comes to phones that not only communicate but can broadcast my every move, tell time, take pictures, and report the weather. Computers are another thing that is mind boggling as it stores my thoughts for posterity and knows my banker better than I do. It drives me crazy when, just as I get something working in my favor and I am writing what I want to tell you, everything suddenly disappears into a not- to- be- seen world. That's when I call David, my computer guru, to bring back my writing from the computer's world of lost words. That's why I have such a poor relationship with this contraption. We don't communicate well without an interpreter, and we argue a lot.

I can't imagine my Mom putting up with this for a second...her few choice words would have whipped that machine into shape pronto.

☙

Did I tell you that conversations, including disagreements, are the results of our interpretation of another's thought? It is the way we compare how we see our world with how they see theirs, and how we feel about the difference?

☙

Did I tell you that what we hear is often not what is said; we are tuned to our own interpretation?

☙

Part 2

Art of Selfishness

"Everything that lives, from the moment it comes into being, seeks its nourishment and continues to seek it. The food of man is emotional and mental as well as physical. He who does not ask, even demand, his right to that nourishment sickens and becomes a burden by the measure by which he denies his birthright. There is no wise unselfishness without basic self-concern, no permanent power for goodness if the organism that fulfills that goodness is limited or injured. *Your duty is to yourself. The duty to others is achieved only by being what you can become as radiantly as possible*"

David Seabury

The Art of Selfishness

The art of selfishness is not art at all but just plain common sense; we know what we need as soon as we take that first gasping breath, and somewhere in those tiny fragile bones we know who we are. It's part of our packaging.

൨

To be "selfish", taking care of our needs first, is nature's law. Have you ever noticed anything in nature that stops caring for its needs in order to provide for something else? Every plant and animal, except humans, will take what they need to satisfy, and when filled, will leave the rest. I find it interesting that humans are the only ones that will take more or less than is needed for their well-being. We are a strange bunch, as animals go; we often don't take what we need so that others will laud our "unselfishness" or we hoard in order to feel powerful and in control. It is not hoarding when we preserve fruits and vegetables in summer's bounty as a safeguard against winter's scarcity, it is a way of taking care of our needs; like the squirrel's need to bury nuts in the fall.

൨

The Nature of Things

We are the only living thing that allows the outside world to determine who or what we are, and then live according to that belief. We, in our arrogance, shame, or fear strain to be what we are not, while we cover the miraculous Self that we are.

&

We humans are part of nature, along with other animals, plants, trees and every living thing. All have an inborn nature, or blueprint, if you will.

Have you noticed that every living thing, except humans, never question the natural-Self or its worth? An oak tree doesn't try to be a dogwood or a cherry an apple nor do they ask permission to be what they are. They just simply grow to their potential; each knowing its worth and receiving all it needs for its maintenance. The resulting gifts, fruit, vegetables, shade, beauty, are given without thought or expectation.

Giving what their core has produced is part of the natural sequence of events resulting from the life blood flowing through them. *Letting go* of what has been produced is the final part of the sequence, insuring the continuing flow of life.

For instance, no matter how many times my grass is cut it keeps on growing, demanding what it needs to reach its full possibility, all the while putting its roots deeper into what supports it. Flowers grow to their shape, size and color demanding their fulfilling without question, and they give their beauty for us to enjoy. Jess and Charley, my two cats, pick and choose whom they allow into their lives, and then expect all the attention due them. They don't give a passing thought as to whether or not they deserve it.

Life energy flows to the demand for it, just like electricity. If the demand is cut off, for whatever reason, life is strangled and existence becomes a struggle. The same rules apply to all nature, including us.

&

Individuality

Ingrained in us is the need to be acceptable and accepted. That is a human need just like food and water. To become integrated into family life, we learn fast what gets us what we want and what doesn't, so we adjust ourselves to get the most of what we need. Later, we move beyond the family and are socialized; we're groomed to fit whatever the norm is at the time. Often in the process, parts of ourself become lost. We hide those pieces of the original self, thinking them not acceptable.

A problem arises when we let the *outer world* determine our worth, and how it will use us. Rather, it's up to us to determine our own worth by recognizing and honoring our individuality, unique talents, abilities, and most important, to recognize our heart's calling. And then to find a need in the world that they will fill ...that is when the world becomes a better place because we are in it.

Self-maintenance is the prime activity in all of nature, but along the way we have forgotten that. The ego, which is a development of human consciousness, has its focus on its worth, which is fed either by an inner world for expansion, or it caters to the outer world, craving recognition.

Drought

I love my red geraniums that explode redness for me to wallow in on a lazy Sunday morning.

Plants, animals and humans spread out when things are peaceful and comfortable, expanding as if they owned the place. But let the atmosphere change and everything...including us...become apprehensive and pulls in, squeezing into a knot.

When the ground becomes parched plants will shrivel their leaves into little balls to conserve what they have and we do the same, shriveling into little balls of compliance. Let a good rain fall and those plants will unfurl their leaves and soak up every drop, expanding into their fullness. It's the same with us; let our Soul be showered with attention and we unfurl like a flower.

Walking Robots

*Desire is important;
"being" what you desire is
its birthing.*

☙

Selfishness has had a bum rap for way too long. It's time to come to terms with this much misunderstood way of Self-care. When we are hungry we eat, when we are thirsty we drink, when we are cold we cover, when we are cut we tend to the wound. But when we're drained dry by the needs and demands of others, we wallow in the praise of our "unselfishness"; all the while our souls are hemorrhaging. The life blood of our Being is sucked out and we live in a coma of compliance.

Being selfish about the care of Self, all aspects of body, mind and soul, insures that the world is made better because you are fully present. That allows your *natural abilities* to provide the source for something needed in the world as well as filling a deep-seated need that lives within you.

There is angst when this impinges on someone's need to keep the old worn ideas in place and to hold everyone to the standard "they" think "right". If you decide to follow that road, you'll find a big ditch to run your life into and it's a hard one to get out of.

There is certainly a need for social behavior or we would be like wild animals. Beyond the cultivation of honoring the rights of others, there has to be a freedom to develop the sense of Being. When that is denied for whatever reason we become walking robots programmed by the past. Robots serve no purpose other than to do someone's bidding. That does not advance the world; in fact, the world is left poorer for the loss of one's abilities to serve mankind authentically, using ones innate intelligence and inborn talent.

Somewhere along the line we are instilled with the idea that we are less important than others. That is not so. Everyone has the right to be here, and there is no one more or less important than you or me or every other man, woman or child…that fact has to be guarded with integrity.

Without a sense of self-importance there is little impetus to advance beyond the ho-hum of what has always been.

Kindness Misunderstood

*I concur whole-heartedly with the person
who said, "No" is a complete sentence
and I try to remember that
it requires no further explanation.*

☙

The word "no" did not exist in my vocabulary. My belief came from the hand-me-down idea that I always had to be available...no matter what...that was supposedly a sign of kindness. Well, It got me all the jobs no one else wanted, like overseeing the making of the dreaded Popsicle stick coasters by fifteen hyper cub scouts needing an excuse to cover everything, including themselves, with Elmer's glue. Or begging door-to-door for support of whatever the arisen occasion of the month happened to be. And there were endless meetings, the purpose escaping in the show of one personality trying to outshine the other. Somewhere in the melee of boredom I began to rebel. Don't ask me how—my enthusiasm just dried up and blew away and there wasn't anything left to give. That's when the word "no" came into my life, and the queen of volunteerism was laid to rest. I felt guilty for letting everyone down that depended on me, and selfish for not doing my "part". But believe me, it was short lived when I found out how quickly I was replaced and without a second thought. So much for being indispensable.

꼬

Did I tell you that giving self away to things that don't interest you is like selling diamonds at a flea market—neither, self or the diamond, will get what they are worth.

꼬

Did I tell you that learning to say "no" to things or people you don't want in your life opens space for those that you do?

꼬

Did I tell you to be kind to your-self…you and everyone else will be better off for it.

꼬

Purpose

There is a pattern to our life, a thread that is started when we are born and continues until, by some internal awakening, it seeks a new course.

You have a purpose and so do I and so does everyone and everything under the sun, otherwise there would be no need for its existence. Nature is crafty in her creations, not wasting a thing. She made everything to serve in their genuineness all other living things.

Earth, air, water and sun give freely what is needed for life to exist. The purpose for that life is expansion…to grow to each potential in order to provide more of what will sustain and advance other life. Everything, from cleaning up the carcasses of road-kill by vultures to using our creative minds to produce and share that which others need to grow and flourish, is the purpose in nature's plan.

If the vulture lays down on his job, dead carcasses would accumulate and the world would be overwhelmed by the stench. The same happens when you don't do what your nature calls for, yours becomes a dead life and the world suffers.

Our part in this plan is to do, be, and give what is inborn as our unique being.

Did I tell you that we are born creators? Our creation might be as small as planting a garden and sharing our roses, or as big as inventing a new use for electricity. The need for roses on a dark, lonely day is no less important than the need for a lightbulb to see in the dark.

Creators

*Our world exists
because we exist, and created it!
And each leaves an indelible mark
that is written in history.*

&

It took a whole lot of self-talk to convince myself that my life had significance in the world. Actually, that thought led me to understand that the only reason *my* world exists is because I am in it, and that world revolves around *my* life!

That took a lot of time and some pretty deep thinking before that made any sense to me at all, and then one day I got it; the world would not exist as it is without my being in it! My children would not exist, all interactions and influence with my spouse, friends and everyone else I interact with would not exist. All the things that have been produced by my thoughts and decisions would not exist, and the same is true for you.

That gave rise to the idea that I am the most valuable person in my life because I am the only one living it: I make all the decisions, right or wrong. In the long run, what-ever this life becomes, it's mine, all mine. Other people influence me, certainly, but I make the final decision. Doesn't matter the reasoning, we all have our reasons, what matters is what I am doing, how I feel about what I am doing, and why I'm doing it.

Did I tell you that *no decision is a big decision* to take what's available or what someone else decides they will allow you to have? Sloppy at best.

The Ego Journey

*We teach others how to treat us
by the way we treat ourselves.*

☙

I use to be "unselfish". Those were my "I-could-fix-everyone's-problems" time of life. My ego was so big that God almighty himself couldn't have done more or better. I was convinced that if I just gave enough, became what they wanted enough, smiled enough, didn't rock the boat enough, and never complained, that everyone would be happy and life would be grand: and I would have made all this possible because I was so very "unselfish".

What a staggering lie that turned out to be. It didn't work then and won't work now or ever. I simply do not hold the key to anyone else's happiness or well-being or, for that matter, anything else that goes on in their life. I am a bystander whose ego has been cut down to size and I have learned to mind my own business, which has turned into a full time job.

Unfortunately, before I had my come-uppance with myself, I was an enabler... a crippler...with all my do-good thinking that was aimed in the wrong direction. I took on what others should have been doing for themselves. I gave money, time and energy like a mad woman out to save humanity. Instead, I crippled people by taking away the one thing that would make them strong...their dignity and Self-reliance.

My come-uppance came when I was told by the person that I was out to save at the time, that he loved his life, loved what he was doing and how; he didn't want it to change. But we, he and I, overlooked the obvious; I was buying his life style while mine was going down the tubes. I smoldered with resentment because I wasn't appreciated, wasn't hailed as the "unselfish" person that I was as I gave and gave.

What is wrong with this picture? How blind do you have to be before you can't see what is right in front of you?

This was one of those sit-me-down-and-talk-to-myself times. I didn't like much of what I heard, but I could see little by little how dead wrong my definition of "unselfish" really was. It isn't, as I thought, giving blindly of time, energy and money, but rather becoming a Self that can use its inner resources to help others see the importance of their own independence and Self nurturing, and, above all else, believing in themselves.

※

Did I tell you that taking on problems that are not your responsibility is a run away ego working overtime?

Here Comes the Judge

"The worth of a cabbage depends on how well it fulfills the promise within the seed. The value of a cow is in her health and development. Service of each lies in this unselfishness. We are no different."

David Seabury

☙

You can't make a move that isn't scrutinized by some inner judge and often condemned as unsuitable. So many good ideas and dreams have been squelched by this inadequate judge, who is self-appointed without a single credential and hands out all our permission slips.

I have been my judge, jury and prosecution, and not very kind ones, at that. The prosecution was relentless in its pursuit to find me unworthy, unlovable and not that good looking either. It didn't take the jury in me long to side with him, and they found me guilty of all kinds of things, from something as small as stepping on someone's toes all the way to ruining someone's life. After I was convicted, the judge in me passed sentence. He took into account every unsavory thought I ever had, plus every time I even felt like looking cross-eyed at someone, and then sentenced me to hauling my heavy bag of guilt on my back. There were many times I was convicted without judge or jury, but by someone else's given opinion.

Something happened when I gagged that judge; the prosecution and jury were out of a job, and I started running my own life with the common sense that I had ignored for so long. Those who were paying the judge under the table, using my self-worth as currency, have all but disappeared.

&

Seems that most every thought we have is a judgment; a comparison of something to something else, someone to someone else, ourselves to everyone else. We judge them good, bad, right, wrong, or somewhere in between. The roles we play in this drama depend on where we are in our thinking and feelings at the time; each situation asks for a different response, and we leave a piece of our judgment behind.

We don't know why people do what they do; we all have our reasons. We do not live in another person's heart, feeling their feelings or experiencing their experiences. We only know our own individual world where perception, tainted by our experiences, does all our judging. It is often out of ignorance of facts that we judge and condemn others as well as ourselves.

Judging is what we do. It is evaluating by comparing one thing against another. This is part of the human evolving intelligence, which lower animals have not yet reached. It is a necessary part of our growth.

Judging is only harmful when we compare self to another or another to self, and find one or the other lacking in worth.

The Craft Show

Many years ago I submitted one of my poems to a local craft show that was being judged by an English professor. I thought the poem was pretty good and looked forward to the results; that was a short lived fantasy when a week later the poem came back with a note saying it was too "sing-song" and received no recognition or award.

I figured that the professor knew what she was talking about; after all she was a professional, an authority, and her opinion had to be right. I stuck the poem in a drawer and stopped writing.

Several years later the same craft show, short on submissions and desperate, asked me to submit something...anything. I thought it a waste of time, but using the same poem unchanged without a thought of winning anything, I submitted and forgot about it.

When the announcement came that it had won a blue ribbon I was stunned. I thought they had mixed up the names; but there it was plain as could be, my poem with a beautiful blue ribbon attached for all to see. I could feel my inside judge cringe, thinking this is a once-in-a-lifetime fluke that can't happen again.

I tried hard not to get too excited as my poem was sent to the next level of competition. I couldn't imagine winning twice, but, when the judging was over and we were allowed to see the displays, there it was with another blue ribbon attached. I stared in disbelief with pride streaming out of my pores. My inner judge started gasping for breath; I think he was having a heart attack.

The final level, where all blue ribbon submissions were sent to state competition, was a big deal, and after an agonizing month of hearing nothing, I decided my ride to glory was at an end.

At the next monthly club meeting my mind was far away, as is prone to happen when meetings become boring, until I heard my name being announced as a blue ribbon winner at state competition. I was so surprised that I began to bawl. I was a mess, but I could have danced in the street. I thought for sure my inner judge would die on the spot.

Can you believe that the same poem, unchanged, won three blue ribbons in three different competitions by three different judges? What one judge with authority deemed not acceptable, three others with authority (also English professors) saw worthy of first prize. That lesson keeps coming back when what I am doing is being judged...I measure it for what it is...just another person's opinion.

꿏

Did I tell you that the neighbor's opinions are ghosts riding our backs with whips that cut deep?

꿏

Did I tell you that not everyone is going to like what you do, but it's a chance you have to take, and hope that, beside you, someone will find it worthwhile?

꿏

Did I tell you to give yourself a pat on the back for the good stuff you've done, and let everyone else's opinion be their responsibility?

꿏

Water Under the Bridge

*Our yesterday produced our today,
and today is the seed
where our tomorrow is hidden.*

❧

I suspect there is a lot to be said about missed dreams, but, they are water under the bridge. Who knows, I could have been what I am not, if I knew then what I know now. But I didn't.

I wrapped my early life around me with old worn ideas that were binding and safe. It allowed me to be what I was programed to become…what most women were programed to become at that time in history…a stay-at-home wife and mother. It was not a bad life; in fact, I loved doing what I did as a wife and mother and home-maker; but doing it, at least in my family, didn't produce a lot of self-confidence or value, it was simply expected.

When I think back to that young, inexperienced mother and wife that I was, I understand that she did the best she could with what she had and knew, and she did it with a good heart and intention.

She, like most of us in our unknowing, was a product of her past. She did what her mother did and probably her mother before her, and so it goes. We seem to live buried in the debris of the past, the old ways that have outlived their usefulness.

That was a long time ago, but without it I would have no memories or history that is the richness of my life. I could not have moved to where I am today without looking back and questioning the reason for my life and what I have learned from it.

ଧ

I try to remember that today's grapes are tomorrow's wine.

ଧ

Reflections

*We are blind to the images
in the mirrors in our life.*

⁂

When we look around us we will see what we think of ourselves; it is reflected in the friends we choose, along with our spouse/significant other, our work, and hobbies. They reflect the life we are living and our feeling of self-worth. We see in them what we have become. We are drawn to certain groups because they give us <u>*permission*</u> to be comfortable with what we do and who we are at the time. They provide a space where we feel a sense of belonging, of being accepted.

If the way you see yourself changes, the way you see everything around you changes. The people, places and things that once attracted you will no longer draw you, and you become uncomfortable with them or what they are doing. That can be intimidating if you feel a sense of obligation to stay with the familiar that no longer fits.

Permission Slips

I used to think it was so much easier to let someone else tell me what to do. All I had to do was follow their directions and life should run smoothly and there would be no angst. If things didn't work as planned it would be their fault; I would only be the innocent victim of their faulty planning.

☙

When I went to school permission slips handed out by the teacher was the only way I got to do anything other than sit down, shut up and pay attention. Often it's the same way today. Instead of the teacher's permission, we are under the thumb of:

Corporate rules...probably made to satisfy the big honcho in charge:

Government rules...a great mystery:

A spouse or significant other...who rules the roost:

Kids...that are trained to feel entitlement, no matter what:

Parents... who think they own you because they gave you birth.

The list is endless.

The role we assume in these little scenarios is usually determined by our patterning and feelings. These cover a lot of territory, from the feeling of guilt, to the feeling of not being enough, and even to the fear for self's survival. The decisions we make are colored by these feelings.

☙

Did I tell you that trying to please everyone is like trying to fill a sieve with water? Both are draining.

☙

Procrastination

> When we commit to an idea,
> the mind is fed like a newborn
> at its Mother's breast.
>
> ತ

I spent a lot of time on mindless doings, the same day-after-day routine that repeats ad infinitum. What I have learned is that the world still functions if I don't make my bed or dust under the couch. Of course there are essentials that I need to do in order to keep body and soul together, as well as the health department from my door. But what I have learned, is that filling my time with the unnecessaries was my way of procrastinating, keeping myself from doing something different because I wasn't sure what different would bring. The unknown is the bogey man that keeps us tied to the familiar, but it's the unknown where all possibilities live.

We often become addicted to the unnecessary...like the need to do everything the same way, at the same time, just because that's the way it's always been done. Sometimes our time is better spent reading a good book, having an unexpected picnic with a four year old, or sharing an afternoon with a friend...those are the things that are life filling and important and make the necessaries easier.

Straddling the Fence

Indecision is a decision
that has no chance.

&

Those who constantly ask your opinion, and then give you fifty reasons why it won't work, are the ones that can't, or won't, make a decision for themselves? I've often thought about this, and I have come to the conclusion that they are afraid of being held responsible for the outcome. They don't trust that the outcome will be what they want and so avoid making a move.

Straddling the fence of indecision is like trying to walk in two directions at the same time. It will surely cut you in two. Decide. Right or wrong, you have a 50/50 chance either way. No decision is a decision that has *no* chance. Once you are sure of the facts in a situation say "yes" or "no" and don't waiver. Wavering only puts you back on the fence of indecision. When you make a choice, act on it without looking back. You cannot see where you are going or what is in front of you when you are looking backward.

Follow your chosen path until you come to your goal or are faced with a crossroad where another decision is to be made.

Be aware, detours happen. It's a part of life's mystery, like roads under construction...life is constantly being refigured. If you come to the end of the road, turn right or left by following that inner call. Don't stop or lose sight of your destination for atrophy will set in. Nature has a way of taking over anything that stands still too long; look how fast vines cover an old abandoned house.

The List Maker

Life is made of lists, each a part of us:

Today I need:

>Potatoes, beans and cabbage, to fill the hunger in my belly.

Today I need:

>Dancing, laughter and song, to fill the hunger in my childness.

Today I need:

>An ear to listen, to fill the hunger in my heart.

Today I need:

>To be alone, to fill the hunger in my soul.

Today I need . . .

LISTS

*Lists are a fine thing
as long as they are short reminders
of the necessary*

I'm a list maker. It makes me feel organized, like I have everything and everyone under control. I check off each duty accomplished as if myself has again won the battle of inertia. It is a rare day when I go to bed with a check on every entry. Some things just never get done. And the funny thing is, the longer they stay on the list, the less important they are; which tells me that it's useless to get too edgy about what isn't accomplished. Of course laundry and dishes have a way of growing if you keep adding without subtracting and eventually you find your underwear drawer empty and the dish cupboard bare. So there are priority lists that keep things moving in our day-to-day; but these are givens and are only added to my list to impress myself with all that I have to do in a given day.

My lists have changed over the years and have become less demanding and lean more toward the important—like my want-tos instead of my have-tos.

I have learned that life is as demanding as we make it. Too many demands make my days exhausting and memories less memorable. Life happens while we are putting checks on our "to-do" list and the opportunity to touch someone's heart or fun bone is lost. Lists are a fine thing as long as they are short reminders of the necessary.

The Dream Life

*You tell me your dreams
and I will tell you mine,
and we will fly together into the
never-never world of tomorrow.*

&

I have also learned that a dream life is not always about accumulating more, such as highfaluting jobs, lots of money and things...all kinds of things. Life's trappings take over and the author of our soul is hushed.

There is surely nothing wrong with having all this, I have honestly had my share, but I found out that things had a way of owning my time, both in the acquiring and then in the maintaining.

The neighbor's approval, even envy, did something for my ego, but they didn't sleep in my bed and wonder why life was so dull.

I believe the real dream in all of us is far more nebulous. It is a longing to create from the core of self. There is a longing in the human heart to contribute, to give that unique something within each Self that will make a difference in the world. When we find what that something is life becomes worth getting out of bed for.

Security

*Taking a chance is scary,
but when you think of it,
life itself hangs by a thread.*

&

Security I have found is hazy. The truth is it's a head job. Money in the bank is like a good but fickle bed partner; it will move on as soon as something more attractive comes along or is downsized by circumstance. Either way your security is out the door. Here today, gone tomorrow is the good job you felt so secure in; and unless you have a zillion stashed in different banks in the world, you are at risk, because who knows which is the next to go? You are vulnerable.

The good news is that you and all the rest of us are survivors; it's part of the packet of instructions that came with us when we were born. There is something inborn in each one of us that does not fluctuate with the happenstance in the outer world. It is our inner knowing that there is a private door within us that opens to the source of strength, intelligence, ingenuity, and the power of awareness; it is all inside of me and you. We will survive, no matter what. The proof is in the bundle of wonderful success stories coming out of seeming disasters and utter failures.

The truth is, we are here for a very brief time and when the "what ifs" get the upper hand in our thoughts we lose the power of the moment. Live this moment the best you know how, with what you have, and the next moment will take care of its own needs.

&

You are born with nothing
and will die with nothing;
All between is on loan.

&

The Art of Change

*Change is not hard;
it's all the stuff you have to go through
to get there.*

☙

Change happens constantly, with or without us. It is only when you are aware and do something differently that your life will change, otherwise, the world around you moves on while you wallow in your shortcomings.

It was not until I moved out of my old way of thinking and doing that the world around me changed and people treated me differently. When I no longer responded to other's every need, when they could fill it themselves, they stopped expecting it.

When I stopped depending on the opinions of others as though spoken through an oracle, I found I had a brain that still cranked when prodded. And when I let myself out to the world, with all my foibles, I didn't die.

You have no idea how freeing that was! Some people in my life disappeared entirely, but each time someone disappeared, someone else came that seemed to fit my life better. For instance, my complaining friends that helped me carry around my bag of complaints disappeared when I stopped complaining and stood on my own two feet. I found myself more committed in my relationships of all kinds, including my relationship with myself. I found out I am really not half bad and most of the time I am fun to be around.

Self Awareness

*We are scared to death
of our uniqueness
because it is different,
and so we reject it.*

&

"Self–awareness is not the same as the minute to minute consciousness of daily life. Self-awareness is a part of ourselves that daily life slides over in its business of supplying outer world needs; and we are caught in the limbo of a segmented existence. Becoming aware of the potential within the Self can be relearned…it is an awakening to what is within and how to attend to it."

David Seabury

Strengths and Weaknesses

*God made this world
for me to play in and then
left the details up to me.*

☙

We all have a ton of both strengths and weaknesses. Recognizing and working with them is so important in getting the life we want. Our strengths are our talents, abilities and heart dreams and come naturally and easily. Our weaknesses are those things we struggle to do or be. They are not only what doesn't come easily, they include the attitudes and beliefs we hold that take away the authority of our inner nature. For instance, an attitude or belief could be "I'm not smart enough, rich enough, pretty enough, or I'm better than, smarter than, prettier than". These are attitudes or beliefs, and they can be changed.

Another type of weakness is that to which we are not inclined; for instance, I will never know what makes my car run, or how to fix it, and furthermore, I have no desire to know. This plus a gazillion other things are beyond my ability and are better left to someone who has the ability and the desire for them.

No one can do everything, and what we can't do easily and well is better left to someone who can, simply because the pay-off in inadequate feelings is just not worth it. Our time is better spent on what we want to do and comes easily, rather than on what we don't want to do and doesn't come easily.

Weakness and strength are opposite sides of the same coin and are of the same material, which is energy, and you get to decide how it is to be used.

Facts Are Facts

We cannot leave ourselves out of the equation in creating our circumstances. We are the star, the lead actor/actress, and producer in our life play.

It's not so much about circumstances, we all have facts of life that surround us, it's more about the attitude we have about those circumstances. I am not peddling Pollyanna idealism, but to dwell on the harshness of life is not an answer, either. Facts are facts. They are the stuff of life, and everyone's stuff is different...none contain all good or all bad, but are a combination of both. Many, if not most, of the facts in our lives were created by decisions we made, probably unconsciously, and can be changed by making conscious decisions and doing some things differently. That's an individual job, and comes from the hunger or need for something more or different.

Discontent

A cold trip to the Outhouse spawned indoor plumbing.

⚯

No one wants to feel discontent. We want to avoid it at all cost. But, it's a necessary. If everything were wonderful all the time we would never do anything to change it, and we'd be bored out of our skulls. Life depends on discontent to drive us into something new. Where would we be if Edison was content to live by candle light or Steve Jobs was satisfied with the typewriter?...we can't imagine. It was their discontent that brought about different possibilities.

Life does that to us, it makes us discontent with it, and then waits around for us to do something about it, to make something new out of it.

Like Edison or Jobs, we must have a passion for wanting to discover what's inside of us that we want to experience... what's in us that wants to shout itself to the world. What we do about that discontent is the fine line between settling for what is, and rousing ourselves to action.

That passion is our discontent. It is the knowing that we are something more than we have *been,* and the desire to bring that something into the world.

We can't laze around waiting for our passion to knock on our door...that will never happen. We have to go out and meet it and drag it, sometimes kicking and screaming, into our lives.

We must stop chastising ourselves for our inadequacies, and figure out our adequacies and how we can best use them to get what we want.

Starting Point

Pick a corner, any corner, and begin.

༄

We have to begin somewhere, everything has a starting point, and the only place is here, the only time is now and the only tool is self. All else is either memory of the past or a nebulous thought of the future…which is being instigated by what is happening in this moment.

Our first step is to take an honest look at what's going on in our life *right now*, and how we feel about it. We need to explore what makes us feel good and fulfilled and what has become obligation, fulfilling the expectations of others.

We live in the world with its demands…that's a given. But, that which makes the world better because we are in it is not found in those outer demands. It is found in the inner sanctuary that is our part of creative intelligence and to deny that is to deny the soul's longing to express, and the world is less for it.

Choosing

*We choose
and the consequences
become reality.*

☙

The life we are living is obviously the one we chose by the decisions we made, but is it the one we want? That begs another question, *why* did I make that choice, that decision? *What* is the payoff? There is a "payoff" in every decision we make or we wouldn't do it. We get something, even out of a dreadful circumstance. We have an inner need that must be met in order to comfort ourselves even in a dreaded situation. At that point we let outer influences take over control, and we look there to fill what is lacking in us.

This will change when we recognize the inner need, the reason for it, and how to deal with it in a different way—taking back the responsibility for our own well-being. That is not selfish; that is just good common sense and the law of nature.

It takes a conscious effort to *want* a different way of life and it takes courage to *do* a different way of responding. This is not a one day fix-all, but rather a process of adding one insight after another, letting them push the old out as the new takes over; it's like allowing heat to take over as it replaces the cold in a room. That's the journey to our inner power and it is well worth the trip.

Forgiving

Forgiving is not forgetting.

&

What this old crone has learned about forgiving has taken a lifetime. I have found that forgiveness is an ongoing mission, not a one-time happenstance. There have been times when I have had daily opportunities to forgive, because unfortunately not everyone sees things the way I do, and so are forever tromping on my expectations.

When it comes right down to it, it is a matter of accepting what is, just as it is, in the moment. Who knows why someone does what they do? For that matter how does anyone know why I do what I do? My good day could be their hurting day and tromping on my expectation was their only way of surviving the minute.

The generic aggravations that are a by-product of daily living are easy to get rid of. It is the heart hurting, life changing actions of someone, especially someone that we love and trust, that are not easy to let go. These challenges take time and a true desire to no longer be the victim of someone else's mistakes, no matter how large or small.

The hurting is within our self and only our self. We become a victim of our own memories and the hurt associated with them; they are our captors and bind us as securely as any prison.

To forgive is to let go of the *hurting* that someone else's action has caused. Those actions cannot be undone; once they happen they become fact. *It is not the happening that is important, but the effect on us that needs to be explored.* Sin is a mistaken use of energy that is hurtful to self and others. Forgiveness is letting go of the results of another's or our own mistakes. It is as much a sin to hold ourselves prisoners to another's actions as the action itself.

Misery is made from an unending list from our past, where lack of self-worth, uncontrolled anger, depression etc. is formed. We each have our hurts, some hidden and some worn like a badge, but all are the burden we carry that stoops the back, stilts the mind, and breaks the will. In order to live a full life there has to come a time when we say enough, and make the decision to put the hurting to rest, and turn the corner to a new way. That is forgiveness. *That is when we no longer allow someone from our past to rule our lives by continuing to live in the <u>effects</u> of a* *past happening.* It is not forgetting---what happened is stored in our memory and is a fact...but rather recognizing how the effects of the experience and the residual feelings have controlled our thinking and our life. We can move beyond that control by realizing that we have a choice; the choice of storing the hurting in the past, where it was created as a part of our history, and moving on, or the continuation of a life ruled by that past. Either way it is our future. This is not an overnight fix, this letting go of deep scaring. It is, rather, a slow crowding out the past by creating a future that we can love.

By the way, it's not just others that create our misery; we do a pretty good number on ourselves. We constantly beat ourselves over what we did or didn't do, said or didn't say. In time we learn that it's over, and dwelling there has not accomplished a thing except our own bruising.

All forgiveness has to happen in the present, which brings us to accepting where we are now with grace and understanding; we're bound to catch on, given enough time.

☙

Blinded

*We can't see what's right in front of us,
it's too obvious.*

❧

While listening to the countless lists of complaints about his life in general, it finally dawned on me that this person carried his grudges like they were an appendage, reviewing them with regularity. I still wonder how he became so blind to the obvious, or at least what seems obvious to everyone but him. I suppose we are all in the same boat when it comes to being blinded by our stuff, grudges and complaints. We feel we have to hang onto them because we would be so naked without them. We can't see what is so obvious because we are too close; like trying to read a newspaper that is pressed against your face, you need to distance yourself from it in order to see more clearly.

❧

What I Have Learned

What I have learned from all of this is to treat myself with some loving kindness by the way I talk to myself and allow myself to be in the world. I no longer wear stuff I don't like or eat last week's leftovers because nobody else did and I eat the crust of the bread because I like it.

When I'm asked to give what I don't want to give, or do what I don't want to do, I have learned to say "no", and not beat myself up with guilt.

I have learned to get off my duff and make decisions. They have not all been prize winners, but they were mine, and the world didn't stop spinning or even hiccup because of them. And other's opinions have become suggestions rather than the yardstick by which I measure my decisions.

I still don't like discontent but I have learned to hoist my antenna and pay attention to its direction; it usually leads me to a solution I hadn't thought of before.

I have learned that security is fickle and can change in a heartbeat. When circumstances take a tumble I have found a private door within me that opens to the source of strength, intelligence, ingenuity, and the power of awareness that leads me to safer ground. I have the feeling that it's part of the packaging that comes with each one of us.

I have learned to forgive life and everyone in it. I have come to the conclusion that wallowing around in someone else's bad behavior, or perceived bad behavior, is not worth the pain and angst. I have come to like myself too much to let that happen again.

I have learned that we have all agreed to come into body for a particular reason-—a mission if you will-—that will help us understand, recognize, and honor the authenticity of the miraculous creation that we each are. And that each one of us is a unique gift waiting to be opened, surprising and nurturing the world.

I have learned that age makes you braver in your living, or at least not quite as squeamish. When you find Pandora's Box that is filled with intoxicating possibilities and crack the lid, it's too late; what's inside oozes out and spreads all over the place, and no matter how hard you try, you can't stuff it back.

I have learned that when someone asks me, "what do you want", I tell them without a twinge, not considering that they have an ulterior motive.

I have learned that I can't get back what I have already spent, and I can't use time that is not in this breath, and dreams don't require 24/7 of life…They just need pieces of enthusiasm for creating. And I must remember that dreams are of what inventors, skyscrapers and mothers are made.

I understand that I am not here to change anyone else, which is an unimaginable load off my back.

I have also learned that the past, every bit of it, is water under the bridge that we can never wade in again except in memory. The future is just as nebulous, living in a fantasy of projections.

The only thing I know for sure is that I am writing this sentence and the next one is a project anticipated in my mind with the hope that it will materialize.

This learning comes one step, one lesson at a time. Like hopscotch, we can't skip over one-zies to get to two-zies; we have to take one jump at a time and have to cover all the bases. We have to keep our eye on the game because when we lose focus or imitate another, the game goes to pot; we either throw our marker out of bounds or jump into the wrong space.

PART 3

*F*INDING *S*ELF

I wasn't lost
I was right
where
I hid
me.

Maturing with Grace

Clean out your mind like you do your pantry, get rid of everything that is out of date, soggy, and has lost its flavor.

❦

Mid-fifties ushered in a time of change for me. It was then that I started taking stock of my days and, while busy, they were curiously empty and uneasy. One day as I was browsing through a magazine I came across several articles on, of all things, "Aging Well and Maturing with Grace". I was curious as to how I would measure up and so I decided to take their test. With the questionnaire they provided I started filling in the columns, positive or negative, on how well I was aging. The conclusion was that, not only was my next breath questionable, but I was also not someone I would want for my best friend. That is not listed among my most flattering discoveries.

The information made me see things I hadn't noticed in a long time...like the baggy grey sweats I wore that looked like Salvation Army rejects. And the people I spent time with, who like me, were carrying invisible bags filled with complaints about our husbands, kids, the neighbors, our latest ailments and what a rotten job others were doing. These facts jarred me into seeing how empty and uneasy I really was.

It's a well-known fact that information is just so much clutter in the brain unless it's put to use, so I decided then and there to do something...anything to make a difference.

I put on my best and went shopping. I felt myself in a time warp, without a clue of what to look for...so I headed for ladies wear at the local mall. A woman there who was dressed like she knew what she was doing led me to all the right places, from foundations to jewelry. When she finished I was overwhelmed; not in my wildest dreams did I ever think I could feel this way again. That's when my inner judge kept questioning my sanity:

"Who do you think you are? Who are you trying to impress, and at your age? Where will you ever go to wear these things? Have you lost your mind?"

These all seemed like legitimate questions, so in my interrogative state I wrote them down.

"Who do you think you are?"

I'm not sure anymore; I remember who I used to be years ago, and I know for sure I am no longer that. But I have this crazy idea that there is something in me that is still alive and needs some looking after.

"Who are you trying to impress?"

I have fooled myself for too long trying to impress everyone else... I'm tired of being a-closet-wanna-be...

"and at your age?"

What other age do I have? It's now or dead.

"Where will you ever go to wear these things?"

If it's only to the grocery, I believe I could reach the top shelf with the added three feet I feel. Groceries though are not what I have in mind. I'm thinking more of places that I don't even know about yet; or, at the very least, a phone-call to someone who thinks of prunes as a breakfast fruit rather than a solution to a well-known problem.

"Have you lost your mind?"

No, I just found it!

☙

The Grubbies

*Look at your history
and you will see your future,
unless you change the present.*

☙

I also found that lolling around in gray sweats feeling sorry for yourself and eating trash for a day is just fine; in fact I think it is important to have a day for pulling out all the garbage you've stuffed in the invisible bag on your back and look at it. After careful inspection, *accept what is and cannot be changed, change what can be changed, and bury the rest.*

It's a wonderful day when you allow yourself to feel all the grubby stuff in life, and when the day is done, you find you are <u>strong</u> enough and <u>worth</u> enough to weed through that stuff, handle what is for your well-being, and get rid of what isn't.

One last comment about my former life:

The people that I spent hours with complaining and grumbling about the unfairness of life have disappeared. A few have changed into interesting companions and the rest faded into the past, better forgotten.

The Simple Things

Life is simple... take what you need and leave the rest.

☙

I continued exploring and came across this statement in the same article:

"life is simple, live unencumbered, be yourself and do what is natural."

To me living unencumbered means to get rid of all excess, all that is not used. So, all the stuff in our house that hadn't seen the light of day in years was on its way out. After the yard sales and having the junkman haul out the last remnants, I didn't feel one tug of remorse at letting someone else worry about the antique chair that I never got around to fixing.

Next was the exit of the things that I saw every day that I didn't like or never used. I was on a mission and with me in that frame of mind, the kids and John made themselves scarce. I was a warrior fighting house-bulge. Grumbling, John lay low with a wait-and-see approach as he put a curtain of protection around what he treasured.

Weeks later after the dust and I settled down, life returned to normal and John admitted that the house didn't feel as cluttered and he didn't miss what went out the door. He was not one for gushiness, so I took his comments as acceptance of my accomplishment.

※

I was serious, I didn't get rid of just stuff, I ended all the doing that ate into my time like a vulture. The solicitors all knew the way to my door or phone number because I was the queen of volunteerism, proving my goodness.

The word "no" did not exist in my vocabulary. How do you say no to your neighbor that hates asking for donations for the cause of the month as much as you hate having her ask?

When I learned the magical word "no" I flaunted it like someone crazed. The solicitors finally got the message and gave up.

"No" is a wonder-word for getting rid of stuff that is life-cluttering, and "no" can also be a deterrent in creating the life you want. You may find yourself saying "no" to something more than the un-necessaries of living. It's the dreaded judge in us that prods us to toe-the-mark and measure up. In my old age questioning I ask, "What mark, what am I measuring up to, and why?"

I cannot tell you how many times I said 'no" to writing, speaking in front of more than two people (God forbid) or saying what I wanted to say, be what I wanted to be, or doing what I wanted to do. My-good-girl voice kept saying, "it's a waste of time...you can't do that...what would people think...don't make a fool of yourself...you're not smart enough"...and the litany goes on.

Yes and no are power words when used at the right time.

Finding Myself

*I wasn't lost;
I was right where I hid me.*

※

When I thought of myself, I saw my reflection in the mirror...brown eyes, grey hair and blah complexion, nothing exciting. I also thought of myself as a wife, mother, housekeeper, friend, and a million other roles.

After digging around in the dusty past like an archaeologist, I began to dig up unrecognizable parts of myself that had been lost along the way, long forgotten. What I found were the fun parts, a great sense of humor, courage, intuition, talents, and those were only the top layer...who knows what lay deeper?

At a certain age we are expected to become "responsible" and do constructive things, like filling the needs of the world. I took that to heart and plowed into becoming the-original-lean-on-me-girl. That's when some people made leaning their life mission.

That's when the judge in me was born, and grew into a big fat bully. He kept me tied to fixing the world by doing, doing, doing. My ego worked overtime thinking of myself as the great happiness-maker, and I became the supply for everybody's needs and wants.

To my surprise I found out that I was not the great wonder that could make everyone happy; which became obvious when they weren't. My constant doing for them was my own ego on a feel-good-trip. I was doing what they should have been doing for themselves. I made them dependent and weak. I was a problem.

That's when I bound and gagged my bullying judge, stopped being so "responsible", and used that time and energy for more exciting things. That's when all hell broke loose in my life and my family and friends thought I had-gone-over-the-edge. They couldn't accept the change. It was exhilarating!

There still seems to be pieces and parts of myself striddled all over the place. Some of them I still want to avoid; they are the ones I keep in a tidy bag in the closet of my mind where I sweep things I don't want to deal with yet.

☙

Memory Box

Somewhere inside of me I found a memory box with a lid. When I lift the lid and look inside, I find the feelings I have today are some of the same ones that I had long ago, even though the circumstances and people are different. That came as a bit of a shock. After all, I've lived a good while, and am fairly bright...you'd think I would have outgrown such childishness.

It turns out that my early years were spent stocking this box with observations and feelings about everything going on around me. I learned then how to do what was needed to keep under the radar...what to say, what not to say, and when to keep my mouth shut. All important lessons if I planned on a pleasant day. I gave up rebelling after I found out that holding my breath until I turned blue didn't work. Mother simply doused me with water and life went on. So much for taking a stand...It was hard for me to get what I wanted and stay in the good graces of my family.

There were nine kids in our family so Mom and Dad had little spare time, and we all learned early to toe-the-mark. I wanted their love and acceptance and was willing to do what I was told, when I was told and how I was told, at least some of the time. As my nickname was "bullhead" you can see that all was not a bed of roses.

We learn to lie early. It's a survival tool, a way of being agreeable to others. We learn how to stuff ourselves into tiny people that will be approved of and then patted on the head with acceptance.

It surprised me to find that I still got mad or hurt or afraid at the very same things that triggered me as a kid. I remember reacting to John, the kids, friends and family the same way I reacted when I was two or six or ten or fifteen; I stayed under the radar saying and doing everything and anything to keep the waters smooth. But let me tell you, there was a lot of turbulence under the surface. I was a robot moving through life trying to make as few waves as possible. With that revelation I decided then and there to can the robot and take up the job of living my own life.

That stirred all kinds of commotion. People that were used to me as I had been were bewildered and upset. But people can adjust, and when they can't, I have to make a decision ...revert back or move on.

It takes guts to even look into our box of history and see the stored feelings that pounce every time they are touched by something happening now. But that's what it takes to move us out of reacting in the same old way to the same old things and expecting different results.

It's not only cracking the lid on the past, but cracking open our Soul's reason for being here in the first place.

Doing What Is Natural

*There is nothing sadder
than a crotchety old man or woman
complaining about what they don't have
or didn't do because of someone else.*

☙

Doing what was natural became easier. What made me self-conscious didn't bother me as much. For instance, speaking in front of more than two people was paralyzing until one day I was having lunch with friends and telling them about some ideas that I had. I realized that, not only were they listening to what I was saying, they were really interested. When I saw that I hadn't been struck dead on the spot, the paralysis left and I was drunk on this new sensation and wanted more.

In my run away spurt of drunkenness I asked if they would come to a class that I was putting together about life. Their "yes" was like a jolt that sobered me into reality, thinking "Oh, my God, what have I done".

That class led to others and gave me self-confidence and a whole new outlook on life.

I even had the audacity to write and self-publish a book...a really bad book, which my family and friends assured me was fine, and bought most of what I had printed.

Did I Tell You?

Did I tell you that even though your past has a big influence on your decisions, it doesn't own you, nor are you bound by it?

☙

Did I tell you that the good is not all good and the bad is not all bad? Understand that memories of experiences are often distorted. We have a way of remembering the *feeling* rather than the accuracy of the happening. The feeling is the seed that impregnates our mind and we respond to the thoughts that sprout from that.

☙

Did I tell you that it's a given that we all get up, put on our shoes and do what needs doing, that's important, it keeps a roof over our head, and food on the table. But in the dark of night, if an empty feeling crawls in bed with you, something inside is not being fed. That something is the innate core of your soul that longs to be recognized, heard, and brought out of hiding.

☙

Did I tell you that saying yes to the things that make you giddy with anticipation, is every bit as important as saying no to the things that keep you from it?

☙

Did I tell you that every once in a while you have to stop and take inventory of your life? Mind, body and spirit each have their foibles that bear watching as they can get out of hand when you're not looking. The quality of your life depends on it... it really, honestly does.

☙

Did I tell you that it is imperative to be free enough to think what you think, feel what you feel, and be your uniqueness and not another person's interpretation of you?

☙

Did I tell you that you can't make anyone else happy? You can only be a mirror for happiness.

☙

Did I tell you that when the garbage in your life smells bad enough, you'll get rid of it?

☙

Did I tell you that there is no such thing as too late? It doesn't matter the age...where you are is where you are, and if you're still breathing, life is waiting. Fill it with the truth in your soul, or you will die without knowing the thrill of hearing your own heart song.

☙

Did I tell you that hours have a way of slipping into years without our notice, and our dreams slide by with hardly a whimper?

☙

Did I tell you that digging into self is like digging into ivy; pull one end and you get ten feet that is tangled and rooted around everything it has touched?

☙

Did I tell you that when you hide behind a mask and become a clone of society's thinking, you rob me and the rest of the world of the precious gift that you are?

☙

Did I tell you to be different, be unique, be comfortable in your own skin? The person living there deserves your love, and needs to be told often how great you are.

❦

Did I tell you that we give out our thoughts and those thoughts will be mauled and sorted like old clothes? Some will be used, some stored, the rest thrown to the wind like tinsel off an old Christmas tree.

❦

Did I tell you that without you in it, the world would not be as beautiful? *It's true.*

❦

Work in Progress

I gave the grouch in me the boot and replaced him with a more lenient judge, who turns a blind eye to my many idiosyncrasies. That's when I found out that it wasn't you that I was afraid of after all, it was the inability to accept and believe in me as I am. That is still a work in progress, but I see a glimmer of light at the end of that very long tunnel.

Part 4

Aging

Age, a friend of mine, teaches like a mighty sage...exuding wisdom out of the bottomless well of experience.

☙

Life's Vacuum

There go our days,
down the hole of time,
and we are not aware of them
sliding out of sight.

☙

Life, it seems, is a vacuum. I turned around and was suddenly sucked into next week and have no idea how I got there. It has dawned on me that I have sucked up days, months, and years, and have landed at the back-end of old age. How many times have I driven a familiar route, not remembering anything, not even what I was thinking or where I was going...like a spell had been cast and I was whisked from one place to another? I suspect that is exactly what most of us do with life as we sit in surprise, wondering what happened.

Yesterday I was a young thing without a thought of time; today I see time as very precious and share it with a sparse hand. Time is like money, it's hard to keep a firm grip on it. I used to cash a twenty dollar bill and it melted faster than I could put it away; today I am a bit more mindful.

My money is like my time spent with people...I dole it out with discretion, choosing with care. Both seem far more important than they used to and somehow, even though my bank account doesn't agree, I am far richer.

Compensations

Aging seems to be the ultimate failure in the thinking of youth. It appears that without that seeming failure we would all be dead.

☙

Aging is a part of life and has some real compensation. For instance, you're always asked to sit in the front seat, you can say you're tired and people believe you, you can take a nap and not feel guilty, and you don't have to worry about your waist...it's a memory. These are some of the small pay-offs.

The big payoff is the satisfaction of understanding: understanding what's important and what is not. Loving deeply is important, what someone looks like is not. Another's perception is important; the language they speak is not. What we are doing is important, what we did is not.

I also understand that I am taking up space in this world and the rent I owe is paid in living fully and with appreciation. These things are important.

☙

Transient Youth

Just as soon as you think she's yours, she'll turn her back on you. She's fickle that way.

೧

It seems to me that way too much emphasis is spent on trying to hang onto something as ephemeral as youth with nips, tucks, Botox, and other assorted tortures; and all the while time is doing its dance, erasing the results. Not that I didn't come kicking and screaming into maturity, but once here and looking back, the alternative is stark, indeed.

What I have learned is that aging is unavoidable. We can accept the pros and cons or waste precious time in the agony of the unavoidable failure of youth.

Some of the most beautiful, youthful, futuristic people of our time, at first meeting would not be considered either young or beautiful, but as their very presence exudes both, what they look like goes unnoticed. They become our mentors, the one we want to be like when we grow up.

೧

Our Bodies

A miracle, taken for granted.

☙

Our body is going to be around for the duration, so we have to treat it with kindness, but authority, for if you cut it too much slack it becomes lazy and uncooperative.

Sometimes we take better care of our cars than we do our bodies. We need to pay attention and service our body like we would a Rolls Royce: feed it good nourishing fuel, have a regular tune up, and have our motor checked on a regular basis. We need to oil all the pieces and parts often with laughter and satisfaction, so they don't creak and groan. And when the warning light comes on, pay attention; figure out what needs fixing and have it fixed. In time it will get some dings and scratches and become a bit weather beaten; that is acceptable. Remember it gets you where you want to go and the trip is more enjoyable when everything runs smoothly.

These bodies of ours are miracles more intricate than the most advanced world vehicle, and are loaned to us for an incredible trip into the unexplored realm of possibilities.

There is no getting away from it, our bodies change to match the stages of our life. They have different needs at different times and look differently, and the more we deny either the more unsettled we become.

The angst for me was struggling to keep up with what I usta-could and I felt drop-dead tired all the time. I wasn't much fun and neither was life. Everything turned for the better when I stopped being what I wasn't anymore, and started being what I was. I found that what I was missing was much better than what I was trying to hang onto.

Reflections

*Time walks on silent feet
and leaves change in its wake*

☙

Clean store windows have a way of bringing me to attention. I am startled out of my complacency by the reflection staring back at me, a stranger in my clothes. I thought it was just yesterday that I walked by this very same window, and I swear, I was taller and thinner, much thinner, and had auburn hair, and my face was smooth and pretty. What happened while I was sleeping? It seems that time walked on silent feet and left changes in its wake.

I believe if that stranger in the reflection could speak to those changes, she would talk of the stooped shoulders that carried someone over hard times, the wrinkles that formed from good time laughter and sad time tears, the tired eyes that have looked on incredible beauty and unimaginable ugliness, and how those hands have held life and death. I can only give thanks to that woman for allowing me to leave my mark on the world, as small as it might be.

Ageless

Being ageless is my most freeing discovery. I discovered that even though my body has aged *I* have not. *I* live in my body, which has allowed me to experience this extraordinary journey of life, not only by carrying me but by being the barometer of my feelings and the source of my physical senses. I found I am the thinker, decider and gateway for the Life Force; which gives me a lot of leeway in doing what my heart calls for. Even though my body has aged and sometimes doesn't go along with everything I have in mind, we have learned to adjust. We, my body and I, have come to an agreement that some things are just going to have to stay; like, loving, laughing people, feeling awe at stars and sunrises and sunsets, and loving books, as well as sharing a glass of wine on a five o'clock afternoon.

Tomorrow's Seed

Words are done, deeds are done,
the harvest is in.
From the first raw breath
to the soft laying down of life
we leave patches of ourselves,
forming the design of our life quilt.
Each patch is different,
some are dark, some light,
some are gay, some drab,
some are small, others large,
but all are stitched together
with the thread of our days.
Our quilt, like a farmer's field,
has patches that are planted,
nourished and harvested
providing seed for tomorrow.

Some Last Thoughts

The earth is blessed because you are in it. You leave your tracks and they are the measure by which the world expands.

❧

Be like a tree, suck up everything you need out of the earth and into your very marrow, and take the light of the sun into your heart to warm you on your unbelieving days, and the rain to wash you clean of all doubt, and the air to breathe you in your desire to create. This is here for all of us, you and me and every living thing.

❧

Life is a mystery, and like a good mystery, we are held captivated by its twists and turns; we surmise and speculate to the very last page where we find it written, "to be continued".

❧

The Author

Ellie Newbauer

Ellie Newbauer learned at fifty one that life is more than a hum-drum existence and has spent the last thirty five years convincing others of that. She is an award winning poet and speaker, has taught classes on the art of selfishness and new ways of looking at ourselves and our lives. She is currently working on a new book, *Illegitimate Poetry and Other Loose Thoughts*.